Caged

by

Heather Grace Stewart

New and Selected Poems

Caged

Copyright 2016 by Heather Grace Stewart

Photographs by Heather Grace Stewart

Cover & Book Design by Morning Rain Publishing Services

Color Print ISBN: 978-0-9918795-8-8

Black & White Print ISBN: 978-1-988248-00-4

Digital ISBN: 978-0-9918795-9-5

This publication is a creative work protected in full by all applicable copyright laws, as well as by misappropriation, trade secret, unfair competition, and other applicable laws. No part of this book may be reproduced or transmitted in any manner without written permission from Graceful Publications, except in the case of brief quotations embodied in critical articles or reviews. All rights reserved.

http://heathergracestewart.me

writer@hgrace.com

Dedication

For Bill and Kayla, and for my family - for inspiring and
encouraging my poetry
in big and small ways for forty years.

Author's favorite writing tree, Queen's University, Kingston, Ontario. The poem "Jump Start to the Soul" was written under this tree in 1991 when Heather was 19.

Contents

Dedication	3
Foreword	9
Canada Poem	12
Caged	15
Bloom	16
This Christmas	18
Carry Us, Christmas	20
Christmas Prayer	22
We Tweet	23
Risk	24
She Drew Me a Sky	26
Winter Lover	27
Canadian Soldier	28
The Wind	29
Maybe It's Your Love	31
Sail On	32
Human	34
Closer	36
The Path	38
When Freedom Stands	40
On Days Like This	42
Well On Your Way	44
New Light	46
Dead People's Avatars	48
The Waiting Hours	50
Air	52

The Present	54
The Silence and The Sound	58
Hope	60
Finding Joy	61
April Snow	64
Believe	65
Hats	66
Instinct	67
All the Things	68
Preparing to Fall	69
Thoughts from a Gratitude Journal	71
Leap	72
April is the Cruelest Month	73
Be	75
Loving	76
The Journey	78
Promise	79
Dear Daughter	81
Trial and Errors	83
Trending	84
The Gift	86
Places	89
Refuge	90
Artists	91
Sunsets	92
The Fragile Parts	94
It's Like That	96

Beautiful Chaos	98
In the Early Morning Hush	100
Family Growth	101
When She Still Held My Hand	103
Even in the Rain	104
Slower	105
November's Sky	106
Offline	107
The Day You Looked Me In The Eyes	108
To the Lighthouse	110
Symphony	111
Hold On	112
She	114
Carry On Dancing	115
My Love Picks Me Plums	116
Don't Delete	117
The Weight of Living	118
Black Thumb	119
It Is What It Is	120
Cyber Rules	121
Lifeboats	122
We Know	124
The Breakup	126
Be Here Now	128
When You Sleep on the Sofa	129
Every Broken Heart Knows	131
Longer	133

Jump Start to the Soul	134
Poetry Is A Shape-Shifting Zombie	136
Death Toll Rising	138
Guns	139
You Are the Poem	140
Paths	142
Viral	143
A Dear Facebook Letter	145
She Loves	147
Quirky	148
Honest	150
How He Held Her	152
Where the Butterflies Go	153
Wrong Turns	154
Brave	156
Who Said	158
Weatherproof Our Love	160
Maybe We Need to Get Lost	162
Progress	163
When I Finally Make Starlight	164
The Birds	165
Breathe	166
More Books by Heather Grace Stewart:	168
About the Author	169

Foreword

So, here I am. I made it. Twenty-five years as a published poet! I find this so hard to believe—where did the years go? The proof is somewhere in my messy office closet—in yellowed copies of *The Queen's Journal* Arts section, 1991 edition, in the Queen's *Tricolour* Yearbooks from 1991-1995, and in Kingston Ontario literary journals like ASH (Arts Sciences Humanities) which are sadly no longer being printed. Their stories—how they came to be and how I became a part of their creation—remain deep in my heart.

I always loved writing poetry—along a winding riverbank in Kanata when it was still called Glen Cairn, up in a tree fort at our cottage at Green Lake, Quebec, and for the last 20 years, alongside lakes in Lachine and Ile Perrot, Quebec—but it was in those fall days on Queen's University campus in my first year there, 1991, sitting under a favorite oak tree, or on flat rocks along Kingston's St. Lawrence River—that's when I got hooked on reading and writing poetry.

It wasn't long before I was contributing to my first anthology, thanks to an evening poetry group made up mostly of Education students living on West Campus, swapping writing stories with poet-novelists Stephen Heighton, Elizabeth Greene, and Norman Levine at Chez Piggy (lucky me!), reading my poems at Open Mic nights at Grad Club, and wandering the poetry stacks of Douglas Library, dreaming of publishing my own books one day.

I wish to thank and dedicate this collection to everyone who encouraged me in the art of poetry while I attended Queen's

University. Thanks also to everyone I have since met in poetry circles in and around Montréal, to my very supportive writing pals from my Bewrite Books and Winter Goose Publishing days, to Morning Rain Publishing, and to all the readers who encouraged me to turn my *Where the Butterflies Go* blog into my first book of poems, and who take the time today to reach out and tell me they're reading my work.

This collection contains many new poems, as well as a selection of reader favorites from my first four collections, which you have asked to be reprinted here. My 'best of 25 years,' all in one book. I hope you enjoy it and pass it along to a fellow poetry lover. Thanks for all the support—you help keep me writing!

With thanks and love,
Heather

Canada Poem

I want a Canada
less concerned about veiled
faces, more concerned about
veiled truths.
Less concerned about winning
a compaign; more concerned
about uniting a country.
A Canada that includes, not
excludes, one that lifts its
people up,
protects the land,
educates our children.
I want a Canada
that's true, strong and free
like the song I learned by heart
so long ago
when I believed every word
without a doubt.

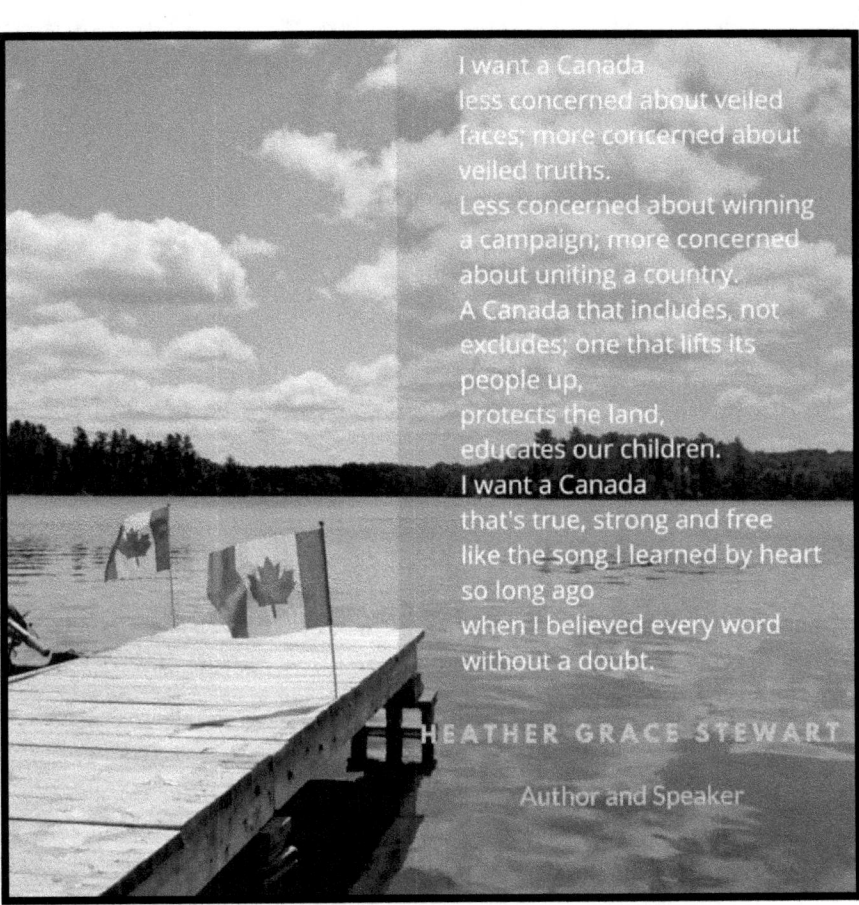

I want a Canada
less concerned about veiled
faces; more concerned about
veiled truths.
Less concerned about winning
a campaign; more concerned
about uniting a country.
A Canada that includes, not
excludes; one that lifts its
people up,
protects the land,
educates our children.
I want a Canada
that's true, strong and free
like the song I learned by heart
so long ago
when I believed every word
without a doubt.

HEATHER GRACE STEWART

Author and Speaker

Author's Note:

I photographed this Amur Tiger at Granby Zoo, Quebec. I was amazed how much the photo came out like a painting. It is not. It is my favorite animal photograph I've ever taken.

I always find it sad to see a caged animal, but when I read that there are fewer than 540 Amur Tigers left in the wild, I got thinking about how this one might not have survived life in the wild, for perhaps he was bred in captivity and never knew the wild. It made me reflect on North American society today, and how we are living our lives; so much 'freedom,' all these 'toys,' and yet so little time to actually stop and rest and enjoy living. That's that's how this poem came to be.

For more information about the Amur Tiger and to learn how you can help conservation efforts, please visit http://www.worldwildlife.org/species/amur-tiger.

Caged

You may stop and stare,
but do not pity me.
I may be caged,
but how are you free?
Chained to your desks
while I play & preen;
You spend half your days
glued to a screen.
I delight in my prey;
I pounce when they sing.
Chained to your devices;
you jump when they ping.
I don't beg for attention.
Selfie? Hear me roar!
Why update the pride
that I just caught a boar?
I owe no one money,
I have no where to be.
Perhaps you are caged,
And I,
I am free.

Bloom

Do what
makes you
bloom

This Christmas

This Christmas, I will be still.
Between the turkey
and the silly paper hats;
between the wine
and the goodnight kisses;

I will find my true North star
make a wish for the world
and count my blessings,
every one.

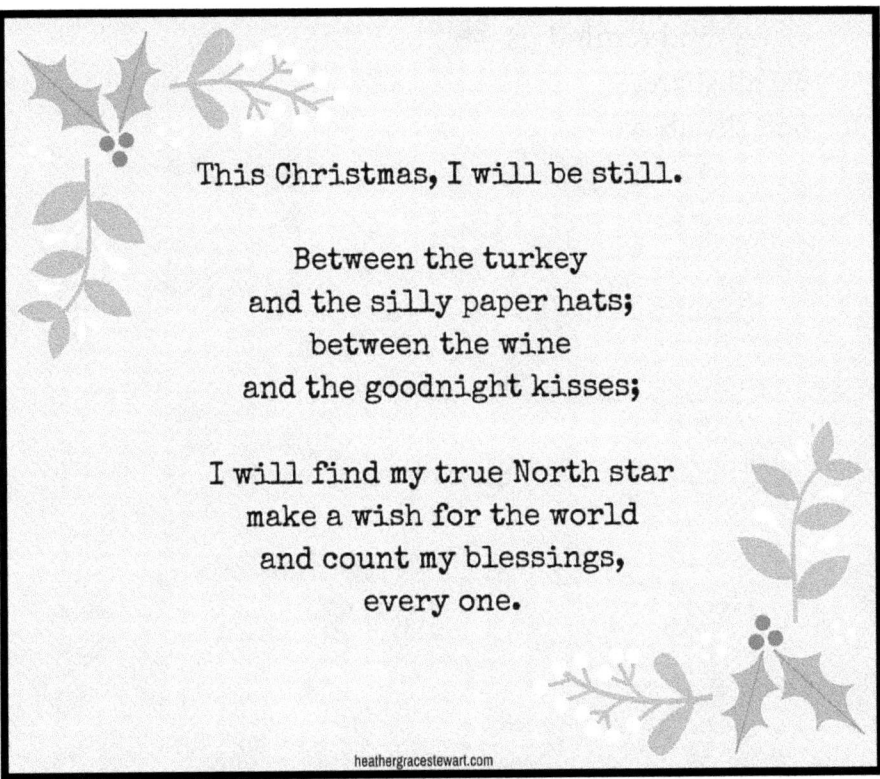

This Christmas, I will be still.

Between the turkey
and the silly paper hats;
between the wine
and the goodnight kisses;

I will find my true North star
make a wish for the world
and count my blessings,
every one.

heathergracestewart.com

Carry Us, Christmas

Carry us, Christmas,
from random acts of terror
to an age of hope and love.

Carry, and remind us—
we all share
one sky above.

Carry us, Christmas,
from random acts of terror
to an age of hope and love.

Carry, and remind us—
we all share
one sky above.

Christmas Prayer

Arms laid to rest,
Peace on the way;
Every child,
a place to play—
Herald that day.

Waters clean flowing,
Fears swept away;
Freedom for all—
Herald that day.

Hatred abolished,
Dreams what we may;
Christmas harbored
in our hearts—
Herald that day.

We Tweet

We tweet to connect,
to say "I was here. I mattered."
All we really need to do
is look a little longer
in our children's eyes.

Risk

Risk something new each day.
Don't be afraid if they laugh because
you are different—
you got their attention.

Be the bright light
that flickers
off beat.

When you doubt what you're doing
or where you're going, stand still.
Just shine, and show gratitude for
where you are now.

You'll know the right direction—
bright lights always find their way.

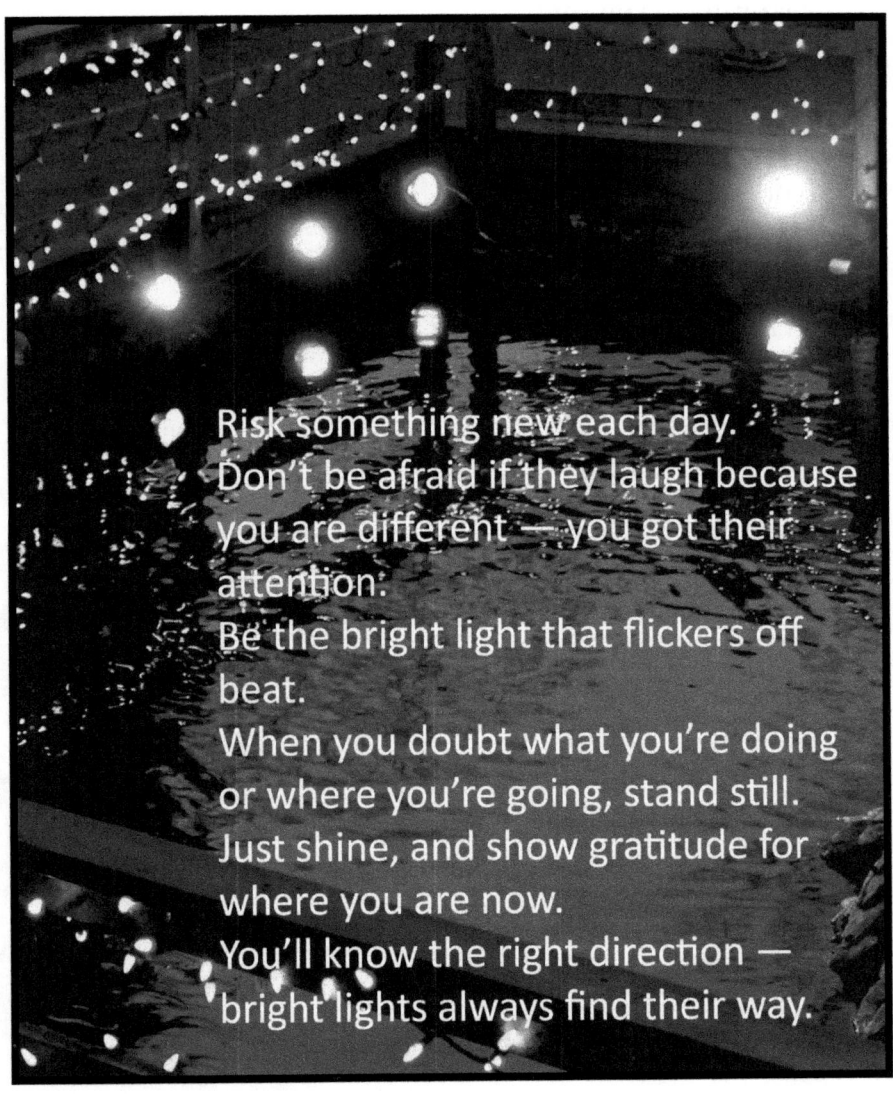

Risk something new each day.
Don't be afraid if they laugh because you are different — you got their attention.
Be the bright light that flickers off beat.
When you doubt what you're doing or where you're going, stand still.
Just shine, and show gratitude for where you are now.
You'll know the right direction — bright lights always find their way.

She Drew Me a Sky

"Mommy," she said,
"let me show you
what I think souls look like."

And she drew me a sky
covered in puffy white clouds.

"There. Can you see them?
They're all around us.

They're everywhere.
But you can't
see them.

If you're quiet, though,
some days—some days,
you can feel them."

Winter Lover

These boughs are heavy, laden with snow—
they don't resist; just shift, lie low.

This world is heavy, laden with hate—
snowballing rage breaks through every gate.

Rest your weary head with me in these hours.
Fade light, fade lies; build us two towers.

This place on my breast will not forsake—
I am your bough; I will not break.

Canadian Soldier

I was a Canadian soldier,
Killed at the tomb of another;
Saluted by my son,
Mourned by my sister and mother.

Don't cry for me, my country,
Stay strong, far and wide.
I was one proud Canadian.
Go live the life
I was denied.

The Wind

The wind is angry today:
a violent lover
throwing slaps against
his lover's face,
branches and balsam
strewn across a
manicured lawn.

I listen to his
sudden rage;
wonder if he holds
the turmoil of the ages
in his fury, in his fists.

Does the wind remember
the agony of that September day?
Does he carry with him
the whispers of Islamic children
hiding from gunfire
inside a cold, dark mosque?

Does he broadcast
the screams of female aid workers
being brutally raped, or the
the suicidal cries from

a young Canadian soldier,
denied medical help
after Afghanistan hell?

No.
If he did,
we'd feel it.
He'd knock us down
to our knees.

We'd be rendered unable
to repeat the mistakes
we've grown destined
to repeat.

We'd never forget.
We'd hear humanity
in the wind.

Maybe It's Your Love

Maybe it's your love
and all this death around us.

But oh my, those fresh peaches
we left on the window sill,
they taste like the first time.
So soft,
so sweet,
surprising.

Like our first kiss,
and this love,
this undeniable love.

How it carries me into my day.
One touch, one word,
I carry on, stronger,
nourished, revived.

One smile, one song,
I carry on living.
Unafraid of

all this death around us.

Sail On

Head up, heart open;
sail on, sail on,
like it's your last sunset.

Human

I think it's so strong to
look someone in the
eye and tell them
everything is NOT
okay. It doesn't make
you weak. It makes
you human.

> I think it's so strong to look someone in the eye and tell them everything is NOT okay. It doesn't make you weak. It makes you human.
>
> heathergracestewart.me

Closer

There are no ordinary days.
Yes, coffee so often gets cold
before you drink it,
work gets trite and tedious,
traffic jams in the same place every day,
love and family fall into routine—

But look a little closer
in that rear view mirror:
There, in that car behind you.
That young girl, her face aglow;
She's on her way to the hospital
waiting to get cochlear implants—
waiting to hear birds sing,
a running stream,
her mother's voice.

Or there,
in that long lineup at the grocery store.
See that woman in the tattered grey coat?
She'll only be able to buy the milk.
Everything else will be put back
and she will walk out in shame;
her three hungry children
tagging along behind her.

Look there, at that big, beautiful home
with the blue shutters.
He's just left her and their children.
Moved away; told her in a text message.
She's feigning an "Everything's Great" grin
for acquaintances on the street,
but inside, she's broken.

How can he erase them
so easily, without emotion?
Erased like chalk-drawn hearts,
not the tiny, beating hearts
they once lulled to sleep.

Look again.
Objects in that mirror
are closer than they appear.

There are no ordinary days.
Not for you, not for me,
not for our angels.

The Path

You are not perfect.

You are a work in progress.

Let go of that heavy load, the expectations you put on yourself, that inner dialogue that weakens you; bloodies you before you even step out the door, on your way to bigger battles.

Let go of everything you ever thought your life would be. Life isn't perfect and you aren't in control. You never were. Let go, and start living. Really living.

Stop running from one perceived priority to the next with no regard for how or why you're running.

Make yourself a priority.

Stop. Sit. Listen. Plant your feet firmly on the ground. Feel the wind on your face; the soft grass beneath your feet; the sun warming your skin.

Feel the heartbeat of humanity, beating inside the earth; beating to remind you:

You are not perfect.

You are on a path. Your path.

You're exactly where you should be.

And you are not alone.

When Freedom Stands

Babies are born and lovers lie;
We'll make plans, when Freedom stands,
Do not let their stories die.

We teach the how, perhaps the why;
Teach to repeat, to ace exams;
Heart and truth would make them cry.

He stayed inside, in search of his brother.
The second plane hit, lens on his mother.

They put on their fire suits, knowing the worst.
They stormed the pilot; called home first.

Some got relief. Some got the wall.
Nine-thousand remains: nothing at all.

Heartbeats skip and minutes fly
like spy planes with capture plans.
And the dead cannot ask why.

It's not the oil. Truly, we'll try.
Allied hands, joining hands—
Empty space in our New York sky.

Babies are born and lovers cry;
We'll make plans, when Freedom stands.
Do not let their stories lie.
Do not let their stories die.

On Days Like This

Sometimes I hold on
too tight;
sometimes I smother.

But on days like this,
the ones below zero,
when you won't let me
give you a sweater and
you're running from me
out the door
as fast as you can

I think, *three days before* Christmas.

He was just a little older than you;
running from rules, from routines,
December's crowded days.

And he slipped,
he just slipped.

They found him floating
face down
three days before Christmas.

Sometimes I hold on
too tight;
sometimes I smother.

But no one really knows
what's waiting
down the river.

On days like this,
the ones below zero,
I pack your extra sweater,
an extra kiss, if you'll let me,

and I let you run.

Well On Your Way

This summer, the sunflowers
grew three times your height,
and you marveled
at what we'd accomplished
in a few months.

But every new day
you grow greater
and don't realize
how much you teach me.

Patience, like when
you draw fine hairs
on your cat drawings,
concentrating, careful
not to erase too quickly
like I always used to do—

Faith, in our world,
in people, even when
so many have already
let you down
at such a young age.

You walk about this world
with a goodness, an honesty
so long forgotten
by the best of us.

It's like you live with
Laura Ingalls in your heart,
and a Minecraft mind.

Keep creating, keep trusting,
keep building.
You are well on your way.

New Light

Beauty grows out of
dark places
when you're reaching
for new light.

Dead People's Avatars

I said I never would
but I just wrote on a dead man's
Facebook Wall.

We're all going to do it
some time.
It's inevitable now.

Dead people's avatars
floating around cyberspace;
their LinkedIn profiles
asking you to join them,
begging you to Invite
them to your event—
despite that they
are dead.

At least it gives us pause
makes us wonder
momentarily if
they're back from the dead —
Zombies are trending, after all —
Or, perhaps we just lost track of them
for a few months
lost sight of them in the nonsense
of our newsfeeds.

So we stop.
And think.
And reflect.
We mourn
a Dead person's avatar.

The living?
We just LIKE
and move along.

The Waiting Hours

How many hours of our lives are spent waiting?
Waiting for hot meals, for late buses,
for the phone call that could make or break our day.

Waiting for the right opportunity,
the right person, the green light.
Waiting for planes and trains,
for good news and bad:

to catch a quick hug at a wedding;
give a final goodbye at a graveside.

I will not count the waiting hours,
or resent them, or will them away.
I wish to embrace them more fully,
like the seconds before a kiss,
first snowfall,
baby's first breath.

The waiting hours led me to you.
They will lead us on
down the winding path
into our next right moment.

Air

The land felt far away.
Was it just an illusion?

I was lost and drowning;
treading water;
searching for direction.

You said my name,
held out your hand,
sat beside me for a while.

You were like coming up for air,
even in the darkest rain.

The Present

It wasn't intentional.
This day of quiet gratitude
just happened.

Power goes out,
comes back on,
lights flicker;
we breathe a sigh of relief
as the future returns full force;
we carry on with our busy days.

Today, I lived inside the flickering lights,
stopped and stood firmly in the now.
I didn't wake up, put on my Sunday best, and
promptly go to church. No. In fact,
I slept in; woke up wondering what day it was.
But by tonight, I had a whole day's grace
to think about, lying awake,
looking out the window at the stars
between me and all my loves:

the ones I miss and don't tell enough,
the ones I haven't spoken to since
last year's Christmas card,
the ones I share this home with

and yell at for silly reasons: *Hurry, hurry!*
The bus will be here in one minute!
You could have called. Supper's ruined.

Oh, so many days, I do it wrong,
but today, I did it right.

When she came to see me
asking how to wrap a present,
I almost said, "It's November twelfth!"
and kept typing my Tweet, but
a wisp of her hair
fell across her face
and I had to sweep it;
tucking it behind her ear,
just so.

In that second, I remembered
how Dad and Mum taught me.
We used a whole roll of tape,
heard Nana Mouskouri
sing Old Toy Trains
half a dozen times;
I loved those lessons.

I closed the laptop and
sat by the fire with her;
her small fingers creasing
the corners, struggling to
get it right; my hands over hers,

gently guiding, teaching;
we laughed with abandon
as we ripped it open
together, many times.

When the shower water
came pouring down
I lifted my face;
felt every drop:
sweet summer rain.
I wasn't making lists or
fuming over past conversations.
The flickering lights were
striking, beautiful;
they made me want to stay inside.

When he called me
to see his handy work
there was no *Just a minute!*
I ran up the stairs, saw his surprise,
kissed him hard. I didn't even see
the sawdust, the boxes still
to be sorted. I was lost
in the warmth of his lips;
in the warmth of our living.

I know you did this.

At your funeral,
the minister kept calling you

by your brother's name.
Those up front corrected him;
annoyed whispers,
awkward silence,
summer heat rising
in the room.

You didn't like your brother much.

Dad and I laughed
all the way home.
We knew you'd sent us a wink.
We knew now: you were fine.

They cut the tumor and
failed, but they didn't
cut your soul.
How you wish we'd live.
How you lived, nearly every day,
until the cancer crept back,
and you simply couldn't see
your dreams anymore.

You sent me this present.

I'll rip it open, every day.
On the days I forget—
make the lights flicker.
I won't sleep in
anymore.

Caged

The Silence and The Sound

You say that I sleep, you say that I've gone,
but you can feel me in the early dawn.

I am ocean mist, I am morning dew;
I am everywhere, and I am with you.

When that old song plays on the radio,
I am the tune and the tears that flow.

When winter snow is falling all around,
I am the silence, and I am the sound.

Wedding day white and baby boy blue;
I am everywhere, and I am with you.

You say that I sleep, you say that I've gone,
but you can feel me in the early dawn.

I am ocean mist, I am morning dew;
I am everywhere, and I am with you.

When that old song plays on the radio,
I am the tune and the tears that flow.

When winter snow is falling all around,
I am the silence, and I am the sound.

Wedding day white and baby boy blue;
I am everywhere, and I am with you.

Heather Grace Stewart

Hope

Hope
hides
everywhere.

We just
forget
where to look.

Finding Joy

I am now in the habit
of finding joy
where it wasn't supposed
to show.

An overcast vacation day,
threat of thunderstorms;
unexpected news by email:
I've lost another friend
to cancer.

Where could joy be found
in the dark morning clouds
that began this day?

Then she took my hand;
led me down a boardwalk—
dewy golden grass
swaying before us:
nature's welcome to the Cape.

Take off your flip-flops, Mommy!
Feel the sand beneath your feet! Now,
watch you don't step on the snails!

She showed me how to move
each one to the side.
Save the snails! she cried
and we did;
carefully naming each
small snail, then moving it
gently from the middle
(certain death by shoes)
off to the side.

Soon they were all
safe in the sand,
under the shade
of golden flags.

Fuck You, Cancer.

FUCK YOU!

We saved small snails
under an overcast sky.

April Snow

The evening news
left us sleepless
with images of protests
in the holy city, terrorist
bombings, drive-by shootings
in our own town.

Yet on Easter morning
we awoke to snow sheets on
a wishing-well roof,
unexpected purple buds
bursting through the frost,
a silver steeple glistening
against the cerulean sky,

and our little girl toddling outside,
to find golden eggs in the snow;
barefoot on icing-sugar-steps,
laughing and dancing
with her sister-cousins.

Driving west at sunset,
morning snow a memory,
the returning geese
called out to us
like old friends,
calling us home.

Believe

I believe in being yourself. I believe in laughing hard and playing harder, and that the true measure of success isn't the amount of money in your bank account, but the number of hearts you've touched in your own unique way. I believe puddles are meant for jumping in, and ice cream should always have sprinkles on top, or at the very least hot fudge. I believe our world is a good and beautiful place that could be better if we all slowed down just a little and remembered where we came from, where we want to go, and to breathe. I believe every woman deserves a chance to pursue her passion, a friend who won't ever let her down, and a dress that makes her feel like Marilyn Monroe on a windy day.

Hats

I love watching you,
watching me,
wearing my many hats.

"Gosh," you say, "so many 'you's."
You say it, perplexed, but
always bemused.

No puzzle here.
No jigsaw to fit:
I'm a woman.
That's most of it!

But why so many
versions of me?
Because you love
and let me be.

Instinct

Golden sunshine shimmers
on this lazy lake
like sequins. A lone cormorant
flaps its wings incessantly,
as if in defiance
of the coming cold.
Oblivious couples walk
arm in arm beneath
the weeping willows,
kicking up dead leaves like
forgotten arguments.
They sport only t-shirts—
the joggers, shorts—
as if wearing them
will prolong
the inevitable: snow
sleet, heavy traffic,
Christmas crowds,
cell-phones ringing
in the middle of a movie.

The cormorant spreads his wings
and praises the sun;
preening on his rightful throne,
unaware that winter is late this year—
going by instinct
because that is
all he knows.

All the Things

All the things
we've left unsaid—
like listening to sea shells;
their secrets stolen,
or long ago dead.

It's no surprise
the tide's come in,
yet we're still wading,
searching for treasure;
for signs, for contention,
for time, for redemption;
and all the things
we've left unsaid.

All the things
we've left unsaid—
like listening to sea shells;
their secrets stolen
or long ago dead.

Preparing to Fall

The day before she started third grade, we went to the park by the lake. I thought it was just for fun, but she told me, as she started running around the play structure, that she wanted to practice for Grade Three, so she'd be strong and ready for "everything!"

She seemed to be enjoying herself, so I didn't question it. The sun was setting on a beautiful evening, and summer had been much too short, as it always is.

As I glanced away from the majestic orange sun setting over the lake and back to my 8-year-old standing on the sand around the play structure, I saw her fall. I caught my breath, but she got up and promptly fell again. This time, backwards.

She fell like a tree falls in the forest. Hands at her side, like a tin soldier. Falling straight back, straight forward, and then, to my surprise, sideways. At this point, I had to ask her what was going on.

"Honey, what are you doing?"

"I'm preparing to fall!" she said with a big grin on her face, and she fell into the sand one more time.

Preparing to fall. Preparing to fail. We prepare our kids to be The Best; to Go for the Gold; if they believe it they can achieve it. But do we prepare them for setbacks? Do we prepare them to cope with failure as much as we push them to succeed?

My daughter had already thought about that, and seemed to have decided that if she was going to succeed in Grade Three, she was going to have to get used to falling. A Lot.

I'm going to have to steal her attitude as I continue trying to finish my first novel, then get it published, then market it. I need to accept and in fact prepare for everything to go wrong. Maybe then, I'll be pleasantly surprised when I finish the race with just a few scrapes and bruises.

Thoughts from a Gratitude Journal

So much seems trivial
studying the sun-kissed tulip
blossoming in the clear glass jar
at my bedside:
be beautiful
stretch toward the light.

Leap

There are leaps of faith
and faith that leaps.

There is transformative power in
a smile, a hello,
an offer of help;
second chances,
chance seconds,
pomp and happenstance.

One man can bring hope
back to a nation
while another condemns
his country to a place
without hope;
without confidence.

What remains are
leaps of faith,
faith that leaps,

and angels all around us.

April is the Cruelest Month

His spirit incites Spring,
running home through
the April snow at sunset,
a seven-year-old adventurer
in PJ bottoms
and flip flops.

Wasn't it just yesterday
I held his hand?
Wasn't it yesterday
I let him wear flip flops
in that April snow?

His spirit incites me.
Now seventeen years old,
walking through our home
with That Girl
who slept over
because we weren't supposed
to be home until tomorrow.

That Girl who says
"Sorry Sir, Ma'am," to us,
slinking past our bedroom door
in PJ bottoms
and flip flops.
Her bra, collected quickly,

hangs clumsily
from her hands
like the slingshots
we played together
before supper
all those April evenings.

As they leave us,
I look out the window.
He has one hand
on her back, so natural,
like how he
held a baseball,
and in the other hand:
three daisies
which he took from
our side garden.

Be

I finally found

happiness

when I stopped

trying to be someone

and decided to just be.

Loving

Less judging,
more loving.

The Journey

A true friend
remembers who you were,
loves who you are,
and travels with you
to who you want to be.

Promise

Today the lilacs opened;
and I almost missed it.

My spring tradition since childhood:
reaching up on my tippy toes,
plucking down a fresh bloom;
closing my eyes, memorizing that scent,
taking out the inner core, sucking
on the sweet nectar.

And I almost missed it.
I was distracted; glued to my computer screen,
stuck on my cell phone, head in the dirty laundry;
Caught up in things that just won't matter
100 years from now.

Then you came home,
scooped up our busy
one-year-old, took us to a little lilac tree
you'd planted in our barren backyard.

The scent was so familiar, a reminder
strong and insistent like your
stubborn side,
damp petals poignant
grazing against my face.

So for a moment it was just the three of us,
carefree and content;
Surrounded by that powerful scent
and the promise of renewal:
The promise of purple.

Dear Daughter

There are a whole lot of things I don't know, but I think I've figured out a few things in my four decades on this Earth, and I feel like sharing them with you.

I've lost four friends who were in their forties when they died (one was a 39-year-old mother of three) and not one of them was a bad person or doing something dangerous. Yeah, people die; sometimes too young. We never know when it will be our time, or when we'll lose someone we love. I know you've heard it before, and maybe it's becoming a tired old cliché, but I don't care, because there is such truth in it: Tell the people you love that you love them now, and do those things you've always wanted to do. Don't put them off. Don't wait another moment.

Try to laugh at yourself. Don't ever allow yourself to say you're 'bored.' Choose friends that let you be your true self. Don't let people walk all over you, but be the person people come to as a listening ear and a shoulder to cry on. Be kind to strangers and give what you don't need to those who need it (including parking spots and that place ahead of you in line). Dance in the ocean, write love letters, walk barefoot in the grass, sleep under the stars, laugh from your belly, take the scenic route, give unexpected gifts. Don't insist on being right; grin and bear it when you want to rip their head off, but do not let anyone disrespect you.

Work hard—not at being the best, but at being your best.

Drink responsibly, drive carefully, love… how do you love someone cautiously, so you won't get hurt, but the same time, with all your heart, so you don't miss out on a beautiful thing?

That's a mystery I'm still working on. Good luck with that one.

Love,

Your honest mother

Trial and Errors

Little girl's joyful song
from the shower
drowns out death
on CNN

Sunlight fades
on another day
we were given
to get it right

Trending

Another Syrian bombing
but the Brangelina breakup
fills our newsfeeds.

PEI is forced to
evacuate its schools
on International Day
of Peace.

I feel lost, unsure
of the right way
to help anymore.

I'm no politician.
I've got few advisors,
unless you count my cats
who lick themselves
and forget
where they were
midway through.

Going with my gut
doesn't work in a world
where the grey has
blurred to bloody,
politics pitch black.

I look to the skies
and wonder if others
light years away
knew the answers,
tried to help us, once,
and gave up,
blinded by the
brightness of
our ignorance.

I'm light years away
from giving up hope,
but we have
much less time
than that.

The Gift

Asphalt-hot July;
feels like a sauna in the shade.
Sweat pours from my brow,
drips down my chest.
I carry a cumbersome bag of
winter clothes, unwanted,
five blocks from our home.
When I arrive, the local
Seconds shop is closed.
I toss the bag into a donations box
that looks and smells like a dumpster;
turn for home.

"Ahh!" says a small voice from inside.
Startled, I look down to meet the eyes
of a malnourished five-year-old black boy,
so skinny, he looks closer to three,
his sad chocolate eyes deep-sinking.
He climbs out quickly, bag in hand;
gives me a three-toothed grin.

"Mamma!" he says. I turn to face a woman
wrapped from head to toe in a purple
African robe and head dress.
"Mamma, she is giving away
a scarf in her bag! A scarf!"

"Mamma" looks at me, then at the goods.
Unsmiling, she wipes her sweaty, soiled
face with the back of her hand and
asks, "You are giving away all this?"—
disbelief in her eyes.
"Well, we need to make some
space in our closets," I say,
shame caught in my throat.

"Here, then, son. You may have these."
She hands him my old scarf, tattered hat,
a pair of dark blue wool slippers.

His eyes grow bigger.
"Slippers!" he grins at me,
then puts them on his
tiny, bare feet. "Are they really
mine, Mamma? For free, Mamma?"

Her pride allows her
one nod, his way,
then mine. She turns,
taking his hand in hers.

He looks back and waves:
hat on head, scarf around neck,
his favorite slippers
on his feet.

Caged 87

"Thank you. Thank you

for the gift!" he laughs,
and the blazing heat
is forgotten.

In asphalt-hot July
I walk home warm,
empty-handed,
richer.

Places

Return to the places
that knew you when
you couldn't tell time;
when you wished
on shooting stars
and spoke to teddy bears.

Let those places
get to know you
all over again.

Refuge

your scent—

not aftershave,
just plain soap
perhaps a touch of
radish and green onion
from working in the
garden—and
every now and then
whispers of whiskey:
a game of pool
with the boys—

stays on your pillow
long after you've left
for work

sometimes
when the day is
slowly choking me
I flop onto
our unmade bed

lying there
in your fragrance
I catch my breath
and carry on.

Artists

He doesn't sit still long
always onto the next project;
building, perfecting, learning.

The benefits to me are twofold:
handcrafted shelves and furniture, and
he gets so engrossed in the woodworking
he forgets to find out
how much I just spent
at Michael's.

Sunsets

sunsets
are
always
free

The Fragile Parts

Life is fragile
and so is love

   we think it, say it all the time
   tell each other we're going to
   spend more time together, less time
   at work/paying bills/reading
   other people's Facebook profiles

   drive slower, eat better, love longer
   because you never know
   what tomorrow will bring

   but life gets in the way
   and we're back to the races
   not enough hours in the day
   to call an old friend let alone
   digest our food, savor our wine
   say 'I love you' first.

It takes a tragedy
to pull us back to the basics,
'Three-year-old Dies Instantly
Hit By Speeding Car
In Daycare's Backyard'

It takes other people's problems
like the couple around the corner
two children under five,
couldn't arrange their differences,
now arranging custody.

Life is fragile
and so is love

of course
you will forget this
in about five minutes
your boss will start
yelling at you or your toddler will
pee on the floor or
your phone bill will arrive and you'll
wonder why, god damn it, you
got double billed again

you will forget about
the fragile parts
and go on surviving.

It's Like That

The best things in life
happen

when you're not looking
for the best things in life
to happen.

> The best things in life happen when you're not looking for the best things in life to happen.
>
> heathergracestewart.me

Caged

Beautiful Chaos

Someday, I'll miss this chaos.

I'll miss the pitter patter of little wet feet covered in dirt and blades of grass, jumping up and down on the newly washed floor, running around the house doing the pee-pee dance, screaming, "Oh no, it's a bumbling bee! A bumbling bee! And also, can we have some juice?"

Someday, I'll miss getting hot and bothered in oh-so-totally the wrong way: wrapping them in scarves and hats and mitts and snowsuits inside a cramped hallway, only to learn once they are all dressed that they have to go pee.

Someday, I'll miss the inevitable post-bedtime, "I want a glass of water!" and, "There's something under my bed!" and, "One more story pleeeeease?"

Someday, I'll miss the grossness of it all: the wiping of little bums and snotty noses; the Puke, Puke, Everywhere Puke, because along with the putrid comes loveliness: the unconditional love of butterfly kisses, of warm, unending hugs; of a small, sticky hand inside mine.

Someday, I'll miss the impossibly early mornings, the insanely late nights, the flu bug the entire family battles. I'll miss all the things I say all-too often: *Don't hit. Don't shove. Share your toys. Eat your breakfast. Be good now. Do you have to go pee? No dessert until you eat your supper. Brush your teeth. It's bedtime. No. I said No. Because I Said So!*

Someday, I'll want it all back. The thousands of digital photos and movies won't do this beautiful chaos any justice. The time is now, and it is fleeting. So when this chaos has disappeared from my life, this chaos I complain about a little every day, I will mourn for it with all my heart.

I will mourn for what I had but didn't always embrace. I will mourn for what has flown away, for what has evolved into something even greater; into something I can only dream about.

Someday, I'll miss this beautiful chaos.

In the Early Morning Hush

When we awake
in the early morning hush
my body curved into yours

I can hear you breathe
as the shadows, light and wind
chase each other from behind
our sheer white curtains

You see me stirring
but just lie there
tangled in the sheets
eyes locked in an embrace as
the sun slowly greets our naked skin

Before the alarm clock rings.
Before the school bus
comes round the corner.
Before the damned garbage truck backs
up with its annoying beep beep beep—

My body curves into yours
just so
and we forget the world.

Family Growth

It doesn't feel like work,
so I never understood the phrase,
"working the garden."

When we work the garden—
Netflix off,
iPads indoors,
cell phones away—
we sweat, grunt, often
burn our skin in the hot sun;
need many litres of drinking water
and our finger nails turn
earth worm black

but it's a labour of love,
so it doesn't feel like work.

He tills the soil with the strength
and expertise of a pioneer farmer;
she thoughtfully places each tiny seed
and fragile plant like a scientist working the lab—
lettuce, green onions, carrots, cucumbers,
radishes, pumpkin seeds and more—
then I cover them, water them, take photos.
Together, we weed, pick the produce,

and chart our plants' progress
mellow yellow summer
into crimson fall.

We plant and harvest a garden,
but it hardly feels like work,
and like the fruits and flowers,
our family also grows
in love.

When She Still Held My Hand

When she still held my hand
my spirit felt lighter,
the world, a little brighter,
when she still held my hand.

Years went by, so fleeting,
with her needing, not needing;
moods like fashions,
boys, oh, the parade of boys—
until one boy
took her hand.

Now I walk alone, yet
warm with memories
of those fall mornings
when she still held my hand.

When she still held my hand
my spirit felt lighter,
the world, a little brighter
when she still held my hand.

Even in the Rain

even in the rain
your face lights up my whole world
even when I don't like you
even in the dark
when we aren't talking anymore
even until death

Slower

slow
your life
just a little,
the voice said, and
in the silence,
answers
appeared.

November's Sky

Meet me under November's sky,
Where you and I are free to fly;
Where time and place do not exist;
Meet me here; do not ask why.

No rules, routines, and not one list,
Just you and I; a gentle breeze;
We'll walk the woods where we first kissed.
No where to be; no one to please.

We'll reminisce; we'll laugh with ease;
You'll say I still have days like these.
So say farewell, love of my life.
But kiss me here, beneath the trees.

Meet me under November's sky,
Where you and I are free to fly;
Where you and I age like fine wine.
Meet me here. One last time.

Offline

the storm slowed us
for a few short hours

layers and layers of ice
cut off cables, canceled plans

so we talked, and we listened
like it mattered
like hearing our own eulogies

and the minutes melted into hours
until the roads were clear
and the world was back online.

The Day You Looked Me In The Eyes

I was walking and texting, looking down,
people talking on smart phones.
Heading to opposite sides of town,
a polluted sea of white, black, brown
drones carrying plastic clones.

Suddenly, our worlds collided.
We stopped buying into lies.
At first, our chat was one-sided,
then talk lived where text presided.
And you looked me in the eyes.

We tossed out laptops, tablets, phones.
Left to our own devices.
How long had we lived like drones?
Wireless, yet lifeless, down to our bones?
We'd become our vices.

A carriage ride through Central Park,
we lay in the grass, looked to the skies,
all day long we felt that spark:
fire on the beach, stars lighting the dark.
The day you looked me in the eyes.

But face to face tired us out.
It's work to connect, we soon recalled.
ALL CAPS, less energy than a shout.

A Smiley, simpler than working it out.
So, back to our gadget clones we crawled.

I'm walking and texting, looking down,
people talking on their smart phones.
Heading to opposite sides of town,
a polluted sea of white, black, brown
drones carrying plastic clones.

To the Lighthouse

Set schedules and spent souls free;
walk along this shore with me.
We're lighthouse lovers;
we're children skipping stones,
in a world of lonely, but
not alone.

Symphony

I miss the days when
you and I were a symphony
and only we
could hear the music

Hold On

hold onto hope
like a Gucci purse
in the subway—

      don't let go

She

She brings me music
a spot of winter sunshine
like the cardinal

Carry On Dancing

You sparkle like early morning sunshine and glitter glue and all the fairies you believe are hiding in our garden, because no one has told you otherwise yet. No one has ripped your wings off and told you…
you can't fly.

But they will.

They'll tell you you're not good enough and the world doesn't work like that. Everyone deserves to dream, but not everyone gets to be an astronaut.

Don't listen to them.

Know your name. Share that sparkle. Make the moves up as you go along. Don't look back. Don't spin full speed ahead. Be in the moment with a dance that's simply yours.

And when you fall—because you're bound to fall—carry on dancing. Carry on dancing like you never tripped at all. Carry on dancing like your final curtain call.

Hold your wings high; use glitter glue when required.

Carry on dancing.

My Love Picks Me Plums

not just any plums, but beautiful black
Japanese plums. I say it's to celebrate completing
our first year of marriage.

Never one to make a fuss, he just smiles and
jumps higher, reaching the uppermost branches,
passing me bushels and bushels of the dark juicy fruit
until they're falling from my hands
and we're both laughing,
blessèd, bound.

(I will file this moment away in my mind
for some day when, in heated argument,
I wish to throw plums at him).

Don't Delete

don't delete the shit poetry

it's still your beating heart.

The Weight of Living

He throws off his work clothes
changes into PJs
helps his girl
fly with airplane wings
and for a moment
sheds the weight of living

Black Thumb

the basil plant
you gave me
told me to try not to kill
smells so strong, so lovely
even as it is dying

It Is What It Is

You don't need to post it,
hashtag it,
take out a billboard ad.
Real friends always find you.

Cyber Rules

find something to hate

hate it with hashtags
hate it without facts
throw in snark for
popularity points

make hate
go viral

Lifeboats

My loves, you are lifeboats
in this sea of change;
you make the journey matter.

We Know

We know we're
emotional, irrational,
unpredictable, and
sometimes, flat out
crazy. We just want
you to love us like that
anyway.

> We know we're emotional, irrational, unpredictable, and sometimes, flat out crazy. We just want you to love us like that anyway.
>
> heathergracestewart.me

The Breakup

The skies are melancholy today.
Even the friendly raven and
squirrels have stopped
their incessant chortling.
The air remains humid;
layers of sunscreen and
salty ocean water.

Summer needs
to say goodbye to us
but doesn't know how.

Should it be fast and furious?
Should it rip the band aid off?
Or maybe give a gentle notification
on our weather apps—
let us down easy:
"It's not you, it's me…"

Summer tries telling
the browning grass,
yellowing leaves,
the cool morning fog:

I need to move on
I need to

but no one
is even listening.

Be Here Now

Be here now
just you and me
under the moon
and the willow tree.
Forget what should
or could be
under the moon
and the willow tree.

When You Sleep on the Sofa

When we've said
all the terrible things;
When we've given up,
slammed doors;
when you decide to
sleep on the sofa

I want to throw away
my Proud Feminist t-shirt
wrap myself around you,
say sorry (even though it
was clearly your fault)

then thank you for
being my person:
thank you for being
my friend
my sounding board,
cheerleader, and the one
who carries my books
to every event.

But, in the name of progress
for womankind
and for our daughter

(even though by now I've
forgotten what made me mad
in the first place)

I carefully cover your toes
with the blue blanket

and
leave you snoring
on the sofa.

Every Broken Heart Knows

Every broken heart knows
that losing a love
is like losing a limb:
you can still feel your leg,
mourn it, yearn for it,
want it back, yet
know it cannot be.

Every broken heart knows
loving again only opens
old wounds:
wounds that bleed internally
keep our hearts and minds
awake at night, tossing, turning,
walking around town like a zombie
in pain that remains for days,
months, years, and
in many ways, always.

Every broken heart knows
tears on the pillow,
sobbing in the shower;
fake smiles on a face, meant to
reassure those who worry;
repeated nods, "I'm fine,"

while the heart is
barely beating,
lungs hardly breathing,
body going through the motions.

Every broken heart knows
it will never fully heal.
And yet, somehow,
it opens itself up again;
a hopeful tulip in the Spring,
joyful at the thought:
perhaps this time,
perhaps,
perhaps.

Longer

Frost webs on our windowpane;
Your skin on my skin;
Warm beneath the sheets—

Lie with me, lover.
Lie a while longer.

Our house lies sleeping, too.
Listen.

Hear that?
Barely audible, or
another sense altogether,

just beneath
our breathing
the humming fridge,
morning traffic—

The dead, they whisper

*No work that will not wait
till tomorrow.*

Jump Start to the Soul

How long will we sleep
uncomfortable
in our own skin?
Wearing woolen mittens wet
because we lack alternatives.

Why do we wait
so long
to live?
wasting time trying too hard
pretending we're someone else's play dough
ignoring ourselves in the process.

At eleven I was my best
at my worst
but never knew it:
climbing trees
catching frogs
searching the soil for worms.

But on cross-legged Sundays
I wore someone else's clothes
Then came the High School Masquerade
and suddenly simplicity
had left my side.

When can we finally
wear our real selves again?
or do we ever   really?

Maybe the answer is only found
in walking alone for a while
in falling down and weeping
in feeling our way through the darkness
of narrow choices:
corridors without a candle.

And when you come to know your truth;
when you finally decide to stop hitching rides and
find your own
true way out of there…

Someone will always
pull up alongside
to offer you a lift
like a jump start to the soul:

Connected to them
you find new courage
to sound your voice.

Then you never think of
all the perfect comebacks
after the insults
because you never walk away
because you never bother to listen
in the first place

So you finally stop whispering
your own name.

Poetry Is A Shape-Shifting Zombie

Poetry is not dead.

It's the walking dead.
Revived from its reality-TV induced coma,
poetry has shape-shifted into the Twitter trending
hashtag: I eat brains for breakfast.
Perhaps the heart of poetry came close to
flat-lined meter and metaphor
over the years, murdered, even,
by MTV, video games, not-so-smart phones,
and with America tuned to the flickering
babysitter every night at eight
who had time for poetry anymore?

We did.
We yearned for a return to simplicity and beauty;
like a champagne glass balanced on a bodacious behind,
we wanted some of that.
Or maybe not exactly that.

So we surfed on, resurrecting the poem,
helping it find new strength
in our tweets, blogs, podcasts, Snapchats,
even in our texts.
You know the ones. Replace the first 't' in text with an 's.'

That's poetry.

Poetry is a devious, shape-shifting zombie, and
it's coming to build a fire under our brains;
to massage our sad, cynical hearts back to life—
because there's no app for that.

Death Toll Rising

Death toll rising;
they search for higher ground,
while we sit here tweeting,
searching for common ground.

Guns

Get the guns.

Grab the guns.
Disable the guns.
Recycle the guns.
Get the guns.

Get the guns.
Destroy the guns.
Make it mandatory.
Stop squabbling.
Shred the laughable laws,
the ones that get made
and unmade
like an antique bed,
depending on who's in office.

Get the guns.

You Are the Poem

You are a poem
that wants to be written;
to love and be loved,
touching the unwell world
molecule to molecule,
leaving it buoyed, breathless,
back to the beginning.
You are the poem
that needs to be written.

Paths

Just another second
in an overscheduled day,
our meeting came and went
without fanfare;
unrecorded.

Across my path
like a leaf in the wind;
Somewhere in between
orange juice and coffee,
business calls and traffic jams,
laundry, e-mails,
dinner, dishes, dreams—

Brilliant red, but understated;
drifting in the breeze.
I stopped to admire you;
you fought the wind,
floated back to me.

Then came a new season:
colors on fire, life
bursting into bloom.

Viral

When I was a kid, viral meant 'sore throat,'
Mom called up the school, or sent in a note.
No texts or messaging, no Snappity chat.
We rang our peeps' doorbells and held up a bat.

Now Chewbacca Mom puts on a mask,
makes a lot of money.
Gets her own figurine. It wasn't even funny.
We debate the color of a dress for days;
When we go surfing, we don't get any rays.

Because now, everybody wants to go viral,
before they hit their downward spiral.
Film something stupid, you never know.
Then tell us how you like fame
on the Late Late Show.

You don't need a great voice,
or a five star review,
to end up in a house with an ocean view.
You don't need talent, or a fancy degree.
Just film your cat flushing its pee.
That'll go VIRAL.

Twerk away on YouTube.
Karoke in the car.
Put those selfies on Snapchat,
so they know who you are.

It doesn't matter
who you are
or what you say, just
make everyone remember to
forget you some day.
 Go Viral.

A Dear Facebook Letter

Dear Facebook:
It's over.
This time it's for good…
Cool! A Fan Page for
Boyz n da Hood!

Dear Facebook:
I'm taking
a cyber-vacation.
(Just let me check
that notification.)

Like a moth to the flame;
it's always the same.
Leaving's not easy;
weekly won't do.
You're using me;
I'm using you.

Dear Facebook.
Deletion.
I think that it's best.
(Why do I have to
submit a request?)

Dear Facebook:
Not fair!

Guilt's not very nice.
"Your friends will miss you,"
makes me think twice.

Like a moth to the flame;
it's always the same.
Leaving's not easy;
weekly won't do.
You're using me;
I'm using you.

Dear Facebook:
I'm sorry.
You win this fight.
Twitter meant nothing!
It was only one night!

Now I'm socially blind—
it's like an abyss—
no viral videos;
no urban myths.

Dear Facebook:
You've got me.
We'll never be done.
I'd miss all my friends—
and Bieber (RealOne).

She Loves

She loves how he looks at her,
the brightest star in his world,
despite that she cooked the pizza
with the cardboard still attached.

Quirky

Quirky
is the new
fabulous

Honest

She keeps me honest
humble
always striving
to be the woman she sees
looking up

How He Held Her

"It's easy, it's just like wrapping a fajita," he joked,
swaddling her four-day-old frame.
Sometimes, he'd hold her like a football
under one arm, and she'd fall asleep like that.
He had a way with her,
like she'd always been in his life,
and because of that, I knew
he'd always be in ours.

Where the Butterflies Go

As the butterflies are beckoned
when fall's frost appears
I will know when to fly
and forsake these fears.

As the southbound monarchs
set off their fireworks show
I will find inspiration in
the diamond-glinted snow.

When the trilliums come to carpet
this old forest floor
I'll be wading in the wildflowers
along some foreign shore.

For when spring brings her wisdom
only then will I know
what I am to become;

where the butterflies go.

Wrong Turns

People will look at you
and think you did
everything right,
bit it takes a lot of wrong turns
to finally find
the right way.

Brave

Sometimes I think
the bravest thing
is just being
yourself in a world
that constantly
tells you
otherwise.

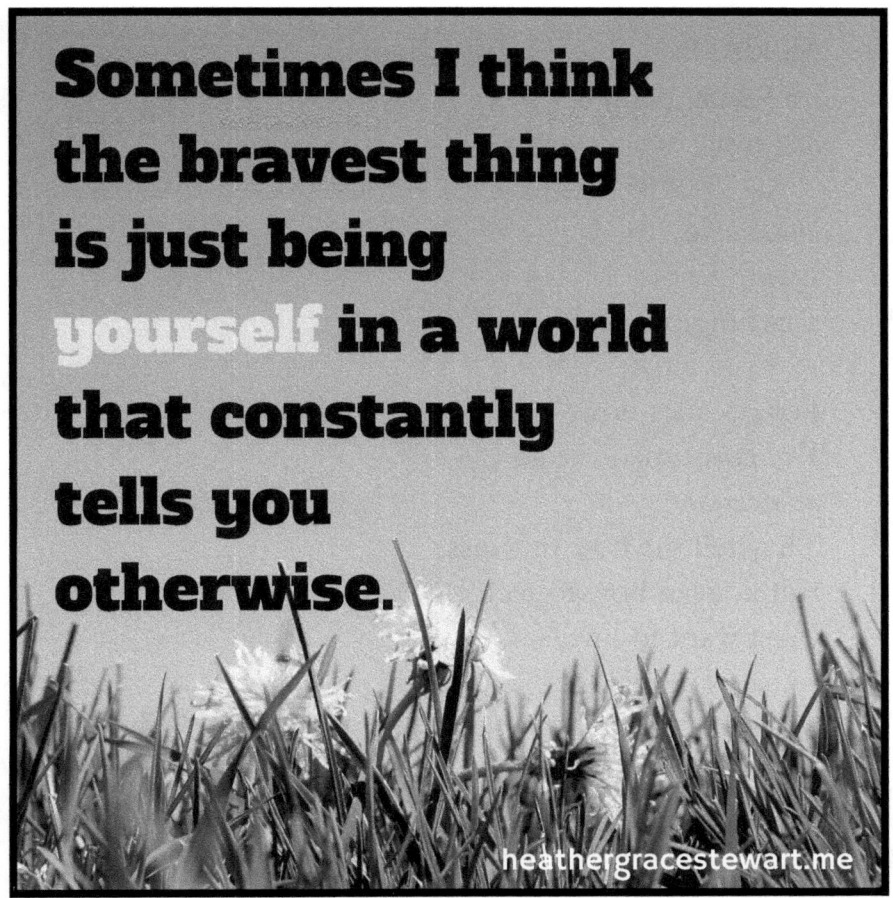

Who Said

Who said
I want to fit in?

Molded like a piece of play dough
into what people
are supposed to want?

Who said
I want to be
anything but me?

For decades now,
I've consumed the ads,
ad nauseum.
They tell me how to dress,
think, even how to feel.
I just want to love.
I just want real.

Who said
alone means lonely?

I'm quite content to
watch the clouds roll by,
count constellations
write words on the fly.

Who said
living was easy?

No way.
It's beautiful, awkward,
painful;
and worth the
price of admission
every day.

Weatherproof Our Love

Everyone laughed
when he forgot to hold her hand
in their 50th wedding anniversary photos
because he was holding a Guinness.

But the point is,
they made it, and we all know
how close to impossible
that is these days.

So many storms threaten lovers:
some just downpours,
over as quickly as they blew in;
others wash everything away—
tidal waves against our vows.

When I watch older couples
going about their days,
the ones holding hands are rare.
Most often, their unforgiving faces
wear unsettled storms.

And I wish we could weatherproof our love.

Slap on some SPF 45 so we don't get burned;
add some damage control conditioner;
a drop of frizz-ease to make

communication simpler;
maybe some night cream to
heal arguments overnight.

Weatherproof our love?
There are no guarantees.
Just hold my hand at 50 years;
I'll give you a Guinness for the other.

Maybe We Need to Get Lost

Maybe we need to piss off the GPS more often. Go off route. Offline. Out of bounds. Stay up until the highway and the gas tank are nearing empty; sleep in our cheap Boardwalk-bought t shirts in a rundown motel with one room left. Maybe we should wake up with no plans for the day, put on yesterday's clothes, ignore the headlines, grab a second danish, find the road less traveled and rough it up; get lost and skip stones on the river under a rickety covered bridge. Maybe it's time to not care, not share, not worry about anything except where we will find our next small adventure.

Progress

She misses perfumed postcards,
snail mail letters;
conversations in cafés
without the words,
"hang on, I have to get this call."

She misses eye contact:
knowing gazes and
flirty glances
that overpower
the urge to send an SMS
or answer the sound
of someone somewhere
logging into chat.

She texts and types
Tweets and Skypes,

then sleeps outside
where stars and
fireflies decorate the
infinite darkness.

When I Finally Make Starlight

When I finally make starlight,
with wired words they will write
my legacy, and get it wrong.
Look for me out in the night.

My legacy is that first song
I sang for you at misty dawn.
You were only two days old;
now sing it to your little fawn.

And the stories that I've told,
they will warm you in the cold,
and calm the baby in his room,
and his baby when he's old.

When I reach the yellow moon,
do not say I've gone too soon.
Sing, and I will shine in tune.
Sing. I will be in the room.

The Birds

The birds still sing,

though I don't know why,

when modern angst fills the sky;

when our oceans are dying,

and our hopes seem dim;

when being good and true

doesn't mean we win.

The birds still sing

an uplifting song—

one of hope and joy—

can they be that wrong?

Breathe

I know it seems obvious, but,
don't forget to breathe.

More Books by Heather Grace Stewart:

Novels:
Strangely, Incredibly Good
Remarkably Great
The Ticket

Screenplay:
The Friends I've Never Met

Poetry:
Three Spaces
Carry On Dancing
Leap
Where the Butterflies Go
The Groovy Granny

About the Author

Bestselling Amazon author, speaker, and poet, Heather Grace Stewart was born in Ottawa, ON, and currently lives near Montreal, QC with her husband, daughter, and three feline friends.

After receiving her BA (Honours) in Canadian Studies at Queen's University in Kingston, Ontario, Heather attended Montreal's Concordia University for a graduate diploma in Journalism. She worked as chief reporter of a local paper and associate editor of Harrowsmith Country Life and Equinox magazines before starting her own freelance writing and editing business, Graceful Publications, in 1999.

In 2008, she published her first poetry collection, "Where the Butterflies Go" (Graceful Publications, 2008). Reviewers call her poetry 'modern' and 'unconventional', the writing 'tender', 'heartfelt', and 'vulnerable'. Additional poetry collections include: "Leap" (Graceful Publications, 2011), "Carry on Dancing" (Winter Goose, 2012), and "Three Spaces" (Graceful Publications, 2013).

In 2012, inspired by the world's infatuation with online relationships, she wrote and published the screenplay "The Friends I've Never Met". Praised by Hollywood actors & producers as 'funny', 'clever', and 'innovative', the screenplay rose to Amazon bestseller status in 2013. In 2012, she also released "The Groovy Granny" (Graceful Publications), a collection of children's poetry, with the help of her then 5-year-old daughter who provided the illustrations.

Following her success of "The Friends I've Never Met", Heather released her debut novel, "Strangely, Incredibly Good" (Morning Rain Publishing, 2014), a contemporary women's romance with an element of fantasy. A year later, the sequel, "Remarkably Great" (Graceful Publications, 2015) was published and met with positive reviews. "The Ticket" (Graceful Publications, 2016), a contemporary romance borrowing its premise from a well-known Canadian news story, topped Amazon charts and has been touted as being "fun and engaging".

In her free time, she loves to take photos, scrapbook, cartoon, inline skate, dance like nobody's watching, and eat Swedish Berries—usually not at the same time.

Want to learn more about Heather? Please visit her at:
Official website: http://heathergracestewart.me
Blog: http://heathergracestewart.com
Twitter: @hgracestewart
Facebook Page: http://facebook.com/heathergracestewart
Amazon Author Page: http://amazon.com/author/heathergracestewart

www.ingramcontent.com/pod-product-compliance
Lightning Source LLC
Chambersburg PA
CBHW071716090426
42738CB00009B/1792